Stone Circle, Jersey, Channel Islands. In 1785 General Conway had the stones removed and shipped 500 miles to his garden near Henley-on-Thames, and placed in their original arrangement! From Old England: A Pictorial Museum of National Antiquities by Charles Knight, 1844.

First published 2017
Text © Hugh Newman 2017

Published by Wooden Books Ltd.
Glastonbury, Somerset

British Library Cataloguing in Publication Data
Newman, H.
Stone Circles

A CIP catalogue record for this book
may be obtained from the British Library

ISBN-10: 1-904263-95-x
ISBN-13: 978-1-904263-95-1

Designed and typeset in Glastonbury, UK.

Printed in China on 100% FSC
approved sustainable papers by FSC
RR Donnelley Asia Printing Solutions Ltd.

WOODEN
BOOKS

STONE
CIRCLES

Hugh Newman

A big thank you to the many 'megalithomaniacs' who inspired me to write this book. These include John Michell, John Neal, Alexander Thom, Prof. Terence Meaden, Jj Ainsworth, Andrew Collins, Jim Vieira and many more!

Image credits: Most pictures are from 19th century sources, in particular Rude Stone Monuments by James Fergusson, 1872. We also lifted a large number of plates from John Michell's great compilation Megalithomania, 2007. Other images are credited where they appear, except those on pages 3 and 47, which are by Emmanuel Martin.

Many thanks to John Martineau and Stephen Parsons for the dedicated editing, picture research and guidance during the creation of this book.

Above: Drawing of Stanton Drew, Somerset, UK, by Samuel Hieronymus Grimm, August 1789.

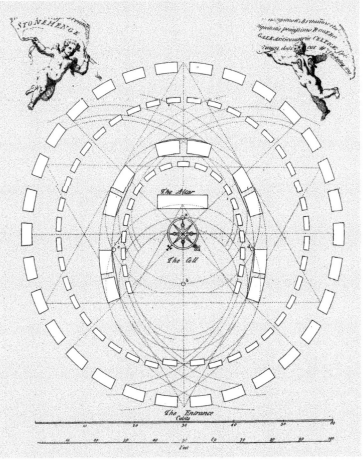

The Altar

The Cell

The Entrance
Cubits

William Stukeley's Geometrical Groundplot of Stonehenge. Published in 1740, this
is the first accurately imagined plan of the site as it would have stood before ruination.

INTRODUCTION

S TONE CIRCLES conjure up a lost world of mysterious ceremonies, druid astronomers, pagan dances and inquisitive antiquarians. The most famous is Stonehenge in Wiltshire, UK, but it is also the most unusual in that it has *lintels* and *trilithons* in its design. Most stone circles are not so glamorous, but with over one thousand of them documented in the British Isles alone, dated between 3500 BC and 1500 BC, their construction was evidently an important part of our ancient culture.

Stonehenge is also well known for its summer solstice sunrise, and research over the last 60 years has shown that many other circles likewise use sky and landscape alignments to mark astronomical events, with many also sharing geometrical forms and measurement systems.

How such mighty rings were constructed has long baffled archaeologists, antiquarians, and other interested parties. In the 1600s, Christians often cited natural or supernatural explanations, and thus the devil, giants, witches and a host of mythological figures all crop up in local construction legends. For how else were such multi-ton stones quarried, transported and arranged with such precision? Avebury is so large that a village today sits within its main circle; its tallest stone was of such magnitude that, once broken up, an entire church could be constructed from it.

Whoever made these magnificent structures had a very deep understanding of engineering, surveying, geometry, metrology and astronomy. And they were not an isolated group of builders—as we will see in the pages which follow, stone circle building was once a truly global endeavour.

GÖBEKLI TEPE
stone circle genesis

6,500 years older than Stonehenge, 7,000 years before the pyramids of Egypt were constructed, predating the agricultural revolution, a vast megalithic complex sat atop the hills near present day Şanliurfa, southeast Turkey. Göbekli Tepe (*see opposite*) was flourishing an astonishing 12,000 years ago and its preserved stone circles (the oldest in the world thus far discovered, numbering as many as 60 across the site) exhibit impressive degrees of technical and artistic skill. They consist of T-shaped pillars up to 20 ft tall, many decorated with animal reliefs (scorpions, boars, lions, etc.) and abstract human forms wearing belts with enigmatic 'H' and 'U' shapes. The taller stones rest in shallow nests on bedrock with small supportive dry-stone walls built in between. In some enclosures two central pillars orient towards a holed stone, the largest and oldest is 65 ft wide. An enormous limestone pillar still sits in the nearby quarry, a staggering 24 ft long!

Over some 3,000 years the circles were filled in with rubble to create mounds, and other circular enclosures built on top. Then, around 8000 BC the entire complex was carefully reconstructed and covered up. Interestingly, the oldest rings are the biggest and most sophisticated.

Like later sites across the world, astronomical alignments are evident. Figures depicted on the Vulture Stone may be the earliest representations of zodiacal and other constellations (including Cygnus) (*opposite, bottom left*). Our earliest surviving building seems to be an observatory, built to track precession, the 25,800-year cycle of the pole stars.

Unusual cup-marks on the bedrock and on top of some of the oldest pillars prefigure British cup-marks, thousands of years later.

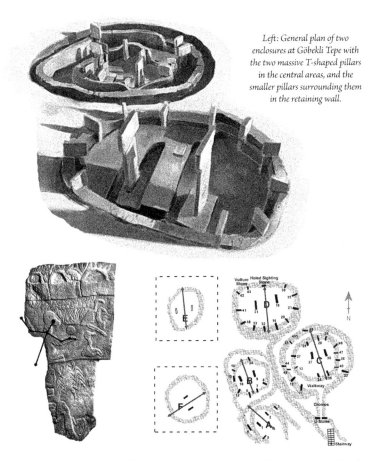

Left: General plan of two enclosures at Göbekli Tepe with the two massive T-shaped pillars in the central areas, and the smaller pillars surrounding them in the retaining wall.

Above left: The "Vulture Stone," showing Cygnus and an orb (Andrew Collins). Above right: Plan of Göbekli Tepe's main enclosures showing their orientations (by Rodney Hale). The later Enclosure E aligns ENE or WSW, close to summer solstice sunrise or winter solstice sunset. The central pillars of Enclosure D align just west of north to Deneb, the brightest star of Cygnus at 9400 BC. It orients through a holed stone.

THE NEOLITHIC EXPLOSION
the earliest megaliths

As we have just seen, Turkish stone circles were being constructed over 12,000 years ago. Elsewhere around the Mediterranean, other early sites testify to similar activity. ATLIT YAM, a submerged semi-circle off the coast of Israel, dates to 6900 BC (*see p. 53*), the earliest phase of the CROMLEQUE DOS ALMENDRES in Portugal (*see p. 44–5*) dates to 6000 BC, and KARAHUNGE (*see p. 52–3*) in Armenia goes back to 5500 BC.

Six and a half thousand years ago, what we now call *megalithic* structures begin to appear in Brittany, France and Britain (*megalith* means 'huge stone'). Ancient British tribes heaped earth upon dry-stone walled chambers to create tomb temples called *long barrows*. These enigmatic sites, such as the WEST KENNET LONG BARROW (*below*), date mostly from the early Neolithic, and predate the much grander constructions like those at Avebury, Silbury Hill and Stonehenge.

The earliest circles in the British Isles, the great boulder circles of Sligo (*see p. 42*), date to around 4600 BC, and monolithic rings then remained all the rage until around 1400 BC, when construction stopped.

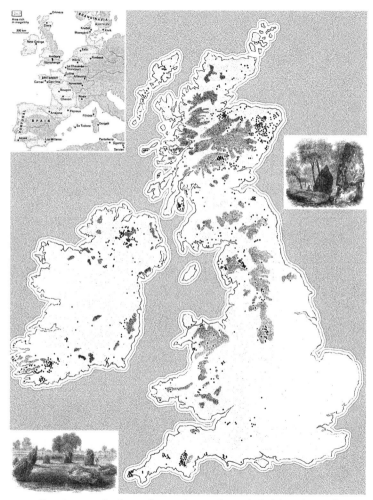

Above: Remaining distribution of stone circles across the British Isles (after Aubrey Burl).

THE ANTIQUARIAN VIEW
some early ideas

The earliest phase of *megalithomania* in Britain was sparked by the English antiquary and writer John Aubrey [1626–1697]. Out hunting around Avebury, aged 22, he was deeply moved by the magnificent landscape temple laid out before him. This and other megalithic sites he visited, most notably Stonehenge (*see p. 18*) and the Rollright Stones (*see p. 26*), are described in his *Monumenta Britannica*, curiously not published in its entirety until 1980. Previously, Inigo Jones [1573–1652] had declared that Stonehenge was built by the Romans and not the Druids, a notion that was not particularly popular (*see his illustration of the reconstructed Stonehenge below*).

The most famous antiquarian was Lincolnshire doctor-turned-clergyman William Stukeley [1687-1765], who traveled the English countryside, illustrating what he saw. He came to believe, like John Aubrey, that Druids were the original builders of these sites, saying of Stonehenge that 'it pleases like a magical spell'. Such theories stimulated the resurgence in modern Druidry that is still evident at Stonehenge and other sites today.

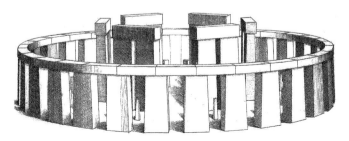

Above: 'The Cromlech at Trefigneth' Anglesea. Near the shore, these dolmens are the remains of stone burial chambers (or barrows) after the outer layer of soil has been eroded or removed.

Above: William Stukeley's 1726 imagined vision of an ancient British Druid.

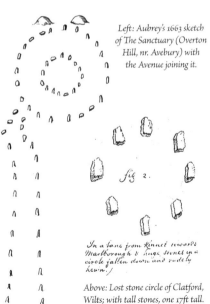

Left: Aubrey's 1663 sketch of The Sanctuary (Overton Hill, nr. Avebury) with the Avenue joining it.

In a lane from Kinnet towards Marlborough 8 huge stones in a circle fallen down and rudely hewn.

Above: Lost stone circle of Clatford, Wilts; with tall stones, one 17ft tall.

CONSTRUCTION TECHNIQUES
hard labour or easy levitation

So how did the ancients build their stone circles? In Geoffrey of Monmouth's 1150 *The History of the Kings of Britain*, a tantalizing legend states that Merlin, in constructing Stonehenge, used 'gears' to move stones from Ireland. The book also mentions giants, and the earliest known depiction of the site (*opposite*) depicts Merlin directing one moving a lintel into place. Unlike Stonehenge, which has beautifully cut stones, some from Preseli in Wales (100 miles away over difficult terrain), most circles are built from rough-hewn stones. However, they still had to be transported, aligned and set in place (*see Richard Atkinson's suggested techniques opposite, and Keith Critchlow's construction below*).

Mysteries remain. At Coral Castle in Florida, Edward Leedskalnin [1887–1951] single-handedly quarried, cut and raised massive blocks of coral, yet his methods remain unclear. In the 1960s John Michell [1933–2009] popularised ideas around the 'earth force'—*telluric* and magnetic currents that might levitate large stones. In the 1970s Paul Devereux [1945–] showed that many stone circles display peculiar electromagnetic and acoustic properties, especially at dawn and dusk.

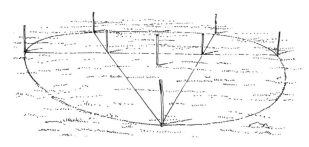

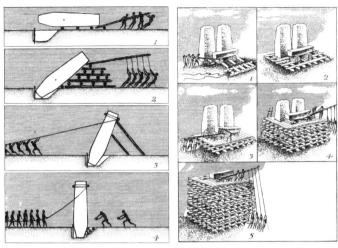

Above: Richard Atkinson's 1959 proposal for raising the Stonehenge sarsens and lintels.

Above left: A giant helps Merlin raise a lintel, from Le Roman de Brut *by the poet Wace, c. 1150.*
Above right: Artist's impression of tribal people moving a heavy stone on wooden rollers.

ARCHAEOASTRONOMY
celestial calculators & cosmic alignments

Discoveries in the 1880s by Alfred Lionel Lewis, and then by Sir Norman Lockyer [1836-1920] and Admiral Somerville [1882-1949], showed that many megalithic sites had astronomical alignments. Lockyer noted alignments within Stonehenge, including the summer solstice sunrise. Then, from 1957, Professor Alexander Thom [1894-1985] surveyed over 300 stone circles (*see pp.12-13*). In his words:

> *Sightlines were ranged from a point in the circle towards the sun at the solstices, equinoxes and other feast days of the calendar, marked on the horizons by stone pillars, cairns or by natural features, such as peaks, notches in mountain ranges or distant islands.*

Thom discovered that the 18.61-year lunar cycle was encoded into many circle sites (*e.g. Callanish, p. 40*), and he also found strong parallels between sites in Brittany and the northern tip of Scotland.

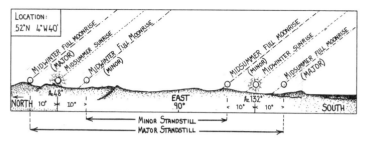

Above: Over 18.6 years the moon's extreme rising and setting positions oscillate each side of the sun's (from SUN, MOON AND EARTH, by Robin Heath). Below left: Today's midsummer solstice sunrise alignment. Below right: Eightfold geometry at Stonehenge (after Gerald Hawkins & John Martineau).

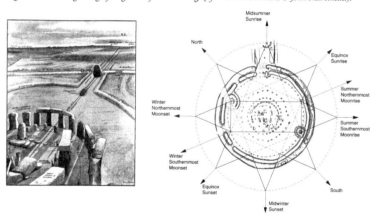

Left: "Nine Stones Close," Derbyshire. A little further south is the rock outcrop of Robin Hood's Stride which may have served as a sacred hill altar. From the centre of the circle the major southern moon is seen to set between the two stone pillars on top of the hill.

MEGALITHIC GEOMETRY
ovals, eggs & eye-lenses

Surveying the stone circles of Britain, Professor Alexander Thom noted six main circle types (*shown opposite, drawn by Keith Critchlow*), and using ropes and pegs investigated how they may have been constructed (in his later work he discovered an egg-shaped circle with a semi-elliptical end). He also discovered a unit, the Megalithic Yard, of 2.72 feet, used in the defining geometry and the perimeters.

In addition to the pure circle it is the almost circular structures, such as the ellipse with two centres and the egg shape with four centres, that seem to have held particular significance for the henge builders. This fact alone prompts us to examine the other shapes more closely as they are far more sophisticated and difficult to create geometrically than the primary circle. [Critchlow, TIME STANDS STILL]

Thom's survey of Avebury showed its perimeter was built of seven curves and two corners (*below left, geometry by John Martineau*), a complex technique we can also see at the ancient circle of MOEL-TY-UCHEF in Wales (*below right*), which is clearly pentagonal in design.

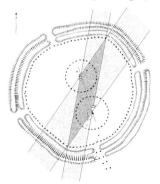 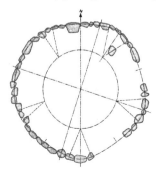

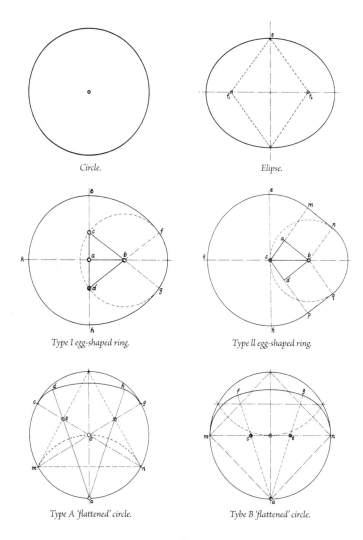

Circle.

Elipse.

Type I egg-shaped ring.

Type II egg-shaped ring.

Type A 'flattened' circle.

Tybe B 'flattened' circle.

ALIGNMENTS AND LEYS
the ancient survey

In the 1920s Alfred Watkins [1855-1935] discovered some interesting alignments between ancient sites. Ley-hunters soon found that almost all stone circles are on a *ley*, their orientation often a clue to another site in the corresponding direction (*see the Silbury ley below*). Some leys stretch across the whole of Britain—the St. Michael Line (*see opposite, top*) has numerous stone circles on its alignment, and the mighty Belinus Line, that runs close to north-south, has some too. Is this merely a coincidence, or was there a great survey in prehistoric times?

The early mapping of Britain is something Alexander Thom pondered, for he had discovered a coherent system of geometry, metrology and astronomy across multiple sites. More recently, Robin Heath has proposed the existence of a great landscape Pythagorean triangle marking important points in the landscape across a large geographic area (*see opposite*). Stonehenge is also connected to Lundy Island and the Preseli Bluestone site in Wales (where an oval stone enclosure called BEDD ARTHUR or Arthur's Grave resides). In 2007, Heath, along with the author and some of the Leyhunters group, discovered a lost egg-shaped stone circle on Lundy Island, very close to the elbow of the 5-12-13 triangle. Other researchers have repeatedly found massive isosceles triangles connecting megalithic sites.

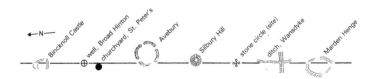

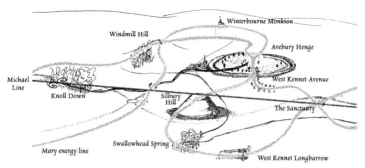

Above: The great St. Michael line in the Avebury landscape with the proposed 'Michael' and 'Mary' earth-energy currents weaving in and around key sites (after Broadhurst and Miller).

Above: One of the many famous leys through Stonehenge.

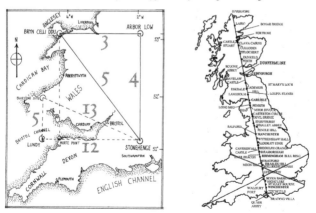

Above left: Two great triangles, one 3-4-5 and the other 5-12-13. These two huge Pythagorean landscape triangles both have corners at Stonehenge (after Robin Heath). Right: The Belinus Line.

WHY WERE THEY BUILT?
what a song and dance

We now know that thousands of people travelled from all over Britain to gather at Stonehenge and nearby Durrington Walls for the winter solstice to meet, feast, frolic, marry, dance, trade, share information and observe the heavens. Compacted earth within other rings supports other local folk memories of people dancing and celebrating. Is this why early Christians were so keen to control these sites and link them with the devil? Right up until 626 AD BOSCAWEN-UN in Cornwall had a reputation as a *gorsedd* (place of judgement), where tribal leaders settled legal matters and discussed astronomy and other sciences.

Many circles have acoustic properties that can enhance and relocate the human voice; some stones, when hit, reverberate. Were these used to affect human consciousness? MEN-AN-TOL (*below*), also in Cornwall, is said to cure sick infants. Research by John Burke suggests that the circle builders were interested in telluric currents and underground water as a way of 'charging' seeds and grains to increase yields. T.C. Lethbridge reported that he got an electric shock when he touched certain stones of the MERRY MAIDENS in Cornwall (*p. 20*). At Scorhill on Dartmoor (*p. 22*), horses were unwilling to ride through the stone circle, and there is a similar account from Avebury in 1823.

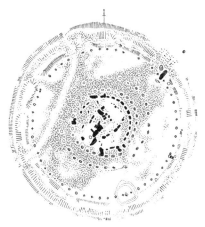

Above: Stonehenge ground resistivity plan, possibly showing telluric currents entering through the entrance.

Above: Mary Caine's "The Giant's Dance of Life and Power" - mystical Stonehenge.

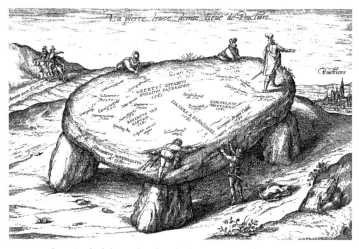

Above: French scholars study and ponder the PIERRE LEVÉE dolmen at Poitiers.

Avebury & Stonehenge
the mightiest megalithic circles

Before we take a tour around the stone circles of Britain and beyond, let's remind ourselves of perhaps the two most important circle sites in the world—both located in Wiltshire.

The great 5,200-year-old AVEBURY henge took an estimated 1,560,000 man-hours and 4,000 people to construct. Over 200,000 tons of chalk was quarried and removed. This is before any of the 500 huge rough-hewn stones were bought from Fyfield Down (several miles away) and erected in the great circles, the AVENUE, and the SANCTUARY (*see opposite and p.7*). Other stone circles once existed within the Avebury landscape, and a second avenue (the BECKHAMPTON AVENUE) once ran from the western entrance of the henge. FAULKNER'S CIRCLE, dating to around 2500 BC, is now just one stone in a hedge. The CLATFORD CIRCLE (*see p.7*), sketched by John Aubrey, had 8 huge stones (one nearly 17 ft tall) on 'a lane leading from Kennet to Marlborough'.

Originally known as 'The Giant's Dance', no other stone circle in the world has a design as sophisticated as STONEHENGE (*see pp. 3, 9, 11, 12, 14, and 17*). Like Avebury it has an avenue, which was lined with regularly spaced stones in Stukeley's days and may once have terminated at stone circle on the banks of the River Avon in AMESBURY. Interestingly, three massive timber posts were erected at Stonehenge around 8000 BC, but nothing further was constructed there until work began on the stone circle 5,000 years later. Excavations have shown that bluestones from the Preseli Mountains in Wales were used in its construction.

Despite its fame, Stukeley wrote that Avebury exceeds Stonehenge in greatness "as a Cathedral doeth a parish church".

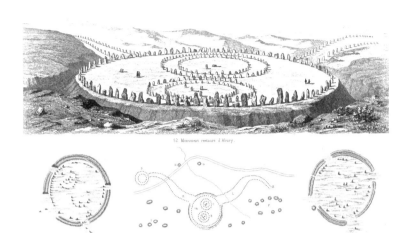

52 Monument restauré d'Abury.

54 Plan en 1722. 53 Plan général restauré 55 Plan dans l'état actuel

Above: 19th century French imaginative illustration of Avebury, showing the site as it stood in 1722 (left), as it stood in 1850 (right), and a full reconstruction (top). Engraving by J. Gailhaband.

Above: Grand Conventional Festival of the Britons. An imaginative take on Stonehenge, 1815.

Bodmin & Land's End
triplets, alignments & lost circles

Cornwall is home to more megalithic sites per square mile than anywhere else in Britain. Seventeen circles remain, with many more lost or destroyed. On Bodmin Moor can be found THE HURLERS, three stones of 26-28 stones, with a recently excavated crystal pathway. The chunky white quartz DULOE CIRCLE is nearby, and the enormous STANNON CIRCLE and the TRIPPETT STONES all share this landscape.

Land's End has several rings of nineteen stones, possibly marking the 19-year Metonic cycle. BOSCAWEN-UN (*see opposite*) has 19 granite stones, one of quartz, which marks the Beltane (May 1st) sunrise from a central leaning pillar, while an outlier marks Samhain (November 1st). The perfectly circular MERRY MAIDENS near Penzance (*see below*) consists of 19 'dressed' granite stones; local legend states girls dancing on the sabbath were turned to stone. Two large menhirs called THE PIPERS sit a quarter of a mile north, and another pillar called GOON RITH to the west. Also in Land's End are the NINE MAIDENS circle of Boskednan and the TREGESEAL DANCING STONES circle near St. Just, the sole survivor of a complex set of stone circles (*opposite centre left*).

Above, with survey below centre: Two views of Boscawen-un, Penzance, a Type-B flattened circle with Beltane and Samhain sunrise alignments. Lockyer believed it was one of the three 'Gorsedds' of Britain.

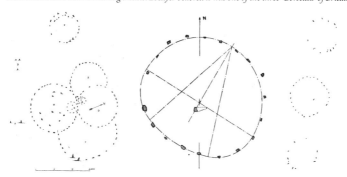

Left: A complex of stone circles near St. Just, now lost, as recorded by William Borlase in 1738. Centre: Type-B geometry of Boscawen-un. Right: The Hurlers triple circle, Bodmin Moor.

Facing page: The Merry Maidens stone circle in 1804. Above left: Illustration of the Nine Maidens in Cornwall by William Copeland Borlase, 1872. Right: The Pipers, two standing stones 13 ft and 15 ft tall.

DARTMOOR & EXMOOR
fairy rows & enchanted circles

Dartmoor is a rugged landscape of rocky tors, waterfalls and wild horses. It also has a rich megalithic heritage. Sixteen stone circles remain, with others dismantled or sunk below the marshy surface, including one discovered in 2009 under Tottiford reservoir. Over 60 stone rows (*see opposite*) have been recorded and many, such as MERRIVALE and SHOVEL DOWN, interact with adjacent with rings. At DOWN TOR, a single row of 174 stones extends northeast from the stone circle.

To the east and south are several large open rings built during the later Neolithic. SCORHILL (*below*) originally had around 70 stones, but only 34 remain with 25 still standing, the tallest at 8 ft tall. After 2300 BC, as the weather improved, smaller circles were constructed higher up, often with more stone rows. The GREY WETHERS (*opposite, the only double circle on Dartmoor*) and FERNWORTHY CIRCLE are fine examples.

Exmoor once had plenty of rings, but most are now gone, and those that remain have very small stones. Two survivors are PORLOCK and the huge WITHYPOOL. Porlock is 80 ft wide—of 43 original stones only 14 remain, and a nearby stone row. Withypool has 35 left (originally 100).

Above: The atmospheric stone rows of Dartmoor; single, double and triple variants remain.
Below: The Grey Wethers double stone circle on the edge of Fernworthy Forest, now restored.
Opposite page: Scorhill, described by Rev. Samuel Rowe as "by far the finest of the rude but venerable shrines of Druidical worship in Devonshire." 34 stones remain, 25 standing, tallest 8 ft.

SOUTHERN CIRCLES
lost, fallen & hidden

The 4,000-year-old remains of REMPTONE stone circle on the Isle of Purbeck were hidden for decades in woods, but their size suggests it was once a major ceremonial centre. Other notable Dorset circles include the oval shaped NINE STONES at Winterbourne Abbas (*opposite*), the 18 fallen stones of KINGSTON RUSSELL near Abbotsbury, and KINGBARROW (a.k.a The Frolic, Easton Druid Temples, or Sawmill)—curiously hidden away in an old limekiln on Portland.

TISBURY in Wiltshire once had an impressive stone circle with a 12 ft central pillar, but it was transformed into a grotto for Old Wardour Castle in the 18th century. Around Avebury, numerous other rings were once evident, but no stones still stand save for one outlier at WINTERBOURNE BASSET. At TAN HILL in All Cannings there was once a tiny circle of nine 4 ft stones, five remain fallen today. Another small circle, 16–20 ft wide with eight recumbent stones was reported in 1923 at LANGDEAN BOTTOM in East Kennet. Close by was HARESTONE CIRCLE.

TWYFORD in Hampshire once had an important Bronze Age circle. Sadly the 'Druid Temple' was built over by a Saxon Church. When this was taken down in 1878, twelve menhirs were found in the foundations, and lie there still; other stones are scattered in the locale.

Kent is famous for the long barrows of the MEDWAY area, but a stone circle once graced the area just to the north. A map of 1869 shows it near the church of Mary Madgalene, but it is absent from later maps. The stones appear to have been redeployed as curbing along an area of green space nearby. Rediscovered by Mr. L. Peters in the 1990s, there are 19 of them, a soli-lunar number often found in Cornish circles.

Above: Stukeley's illustration of the Nine Stones (or Nine Ladies or Devil's Nine Stones), Dorset.
Right: Harestone circle, Wilts, with central pyramidal stone and Samhain sunset alignment.

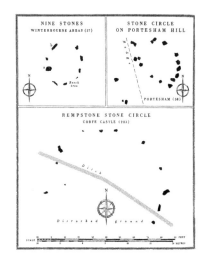

Above: Stukeley's 1724 sketch of the "Double circle of Stones" at Winterbourne Bassett, now mostly destroyed.

Left: A selection of surveys of stone circles in Dorset, published by Her Majesty's Stationery Office in the 1960s.

AVON TO SHROPSHIRE
rude rings in rough rock

STANTON DREW (*opposite top*) in N. Somerset is Britain's finest triple circle and the third most important overall. In 1724, William Stukeley noted an avenue extending from the main circle. The largest circle has a diameter of 368 ft (112 m). Only Avebury is larger.

At the ROLLRIGHT STONES (*opposite bottom*), a complex of three monuments on the Oxfordshire/Warwickshire border, there is one circle of 77 eroded limestone menhirs just over 100 ft wide called THE KING'S MEN. To the northeast is the KING STONE, which, strangely, is in a different county (Warwickshire). Four hundred yards southeast are the remains of the WHISPERING KNIGHTS dolmen.

Closer to Oxford is the 4,000-5,000 year-old DEVIL'S QUOIT, a huge stone circle recently fully restored to its former glory. Its stones and prominent henge can be seen in the image (*opposite centre right*).

Hugging the border with Wales are a few circles. Fifteen stones remain at MITCHELL'S FOLD from an original 30, the tallest being nearly 7 ft. Rumours of a Shropshire trilithon were heard in the 18th century, but later dismissed by Aubrey Burl. The HOARSTONES (*shown below*) has 38 small stones with a central pillar.

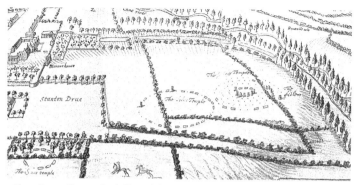

Above: Stanton Drew, as sketched by Stukeley in July 1723. To the west, not shown, is a three-stone Cove, similar to that at Avebury, now in the garden of The Druids Arms pub.

Above: The small, 97 ft north-easterly circle at Stanton Drew, near Bristol.

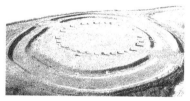

Above: The restored Devil's Quoit. The outer henge is c.492 ft (150m) wide, the stone circle is 225 ft (78m).

Above: The Kings Men at Rollright, built c. 2300 BC, with the King Stone shown in the field behind. The diameter of the Rollright stone circle is the same as that of the Sarsen Circle at Stonehenge.

Peak District & Isle of Man
north to the centre of the circle

Following the ancient trading route linking Avebury with Cumbria, we head north to the Peak District in Derbyshire.

ARBOR LOW, near Bakewell (*opposite*), consists of around 40 limestone menhirs, all fallen. Whether they originally stood upright is unknown. It had a henge and a stone cove, located in the centre of the circle (in contrast to its southern counterparts). Often called the 'Stonehenge of the North', Robin Heath places it within a landscape triangle connecting Stonehenge (*p. 15*) and Bryn Celli Ddu in Anglesey (*p. 35*).

BARBROOK features three stone circles, the main one being a Type-B flattened circle (*see opposite, & page 13*). In patchy tree growth on Stanton Moor, a low stone circle called NINE LADIES (*below*) is located within a grand Bronze Age cemetery. To the southwest the FIDDLERS STONE acts as an outlier, but has been moved several times. The SEVEN STONES of Hordron Edge occupy a delightful position overlooking the Derwent Valley. It had ten stones originally, but three are fallen. Earth lights and strange phenomena have been reported here.

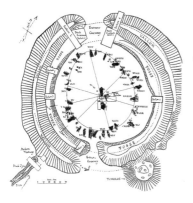

Left, and above: Arbor Low, Derbyshire, with its 40-50 fallen stones, is an impressive egg-shaped circle with a central cove, dated to around 2000 BC. An earthen avenue emerged from its south side towards a huge barrow on Gib Hill.

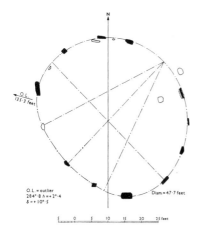

O.L. = outlier
284°·8 h = 2°·4
δ = + 10°·5

O.L.
135·3 feet

Diam. = 47·7 feet

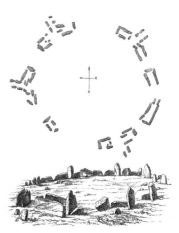

Above left: Barbrook One (A. Thom); Barbrook Two is 300m north with 9 stones and a cairn.
Above right: The only stone circle on the Isle of Man is MEAYLL (or Mull), near the village of Cregneish. Probably a chambered tomb, with six grave-pairs arranged in a circle. Late Neolithic/early Bronze Age.
Opposite: Nine Ladies of Stanton Moor is within a Bronze Age cemetery (drawing by Steve Larder).

YORKSHIRE & THE NORTH
high on the moors

High on the Yorkshire moors can be found hundreds of megaliths, some with remarkable rock art (*see opposite top left*). In the 19th century The TWELVE APOSTLES of Ilkley Moor (*opposite, centre*) was known as the *Druidical Dial*, as it was thought to be some kind of stone calendar. It once had 20 uprights with a central stone made of local millstone grit, but only 12 stones now remain, none taller than 4ft. It forms a perfect isosceles triangle with two other circles, the GRUBSTONES and the BACKSTONES, both 1,300 megalithic yards away, and astronomical alignments have been suggested. Further north is a classic *four poster* (*see p.37*) called the DRUID'S ALTAR near Skipton, sited in the same part of the moors as the APPLETREEWICK, DUMPIT HILL and GRASSINGTON circles.

In the sacred landscape of the Gypsey Race near Scarborough, the RUDSTON MONOLITH (*opposite*) is a staggering 25ft, Britain's tallest. Also of note are the three spaced out DEVIL'S ARROWS (*below*). Between 18–22ft tall they align with the nearby THORNBOROUGH HENGES.

The most northerly English stone ring is DUDDO FIVE STONES. Nearby is the huge ruined circle of HETHPOOL and its smaller sister.

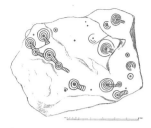

Above: Thom's analysis of the Panorama Stone on Ilkley Moor, near the Twelve Apostles stone circle.

Above: The Twelve Apostles. Balls of lights and UFOs are often reported at this site. After D. Starley.

Above: Rudston, with Britain's tallest menhir, 25 ft;
Left: Cloughton Moor stone circle, East Yorkshire,
with its holed stone; Facing page: The Devil's
Arrows of Boroughbridge, North Yorkshire.

THE LAKE DISTRICT
stone circles as landscape art

Perhaps Britain's most beautifully sited circle, CASTLERIGG is also one of the oldest. Built around 3200 BC, it sits in magnificent open space surrounded by mountains, lakes and an ancient trackway (*see opposite*). Comprising 35 modestly sized stones, it is large, like other Cumbrian rings (108 ft at its longest diameter). Three cairns were discovered within the circle in 1856, and a huge stone axe nine years later.

LONG MEG AND HER DAUGHTERS (*below and opposite*) is the third largest stone circle in Britain. Meg herself, a 12 ft red sandstone outlier, with carved cups, rings, grooves, spirals and concentric circles, sits to the SW on a midwinter sunset alignment. LITTLE MEG, a tiny circle famous for its double-spiral carvings built about 1000 years later, sits to the NE.

SUNKENKIRK at Swinside was a favourite ceremonial centre for pagans in the 1970s and '80s. The grey stones are porphyritic slate, but its function is unclear; no astronomical alignments have been deduced.

Other sites: GREYCROFT, rebuilt in 1949, overlooks the Irish Sea and has 10 of its original basalt stones. BLAKELEY RAISE, a small stone circle, is on the far west of the Cumbrian Mountains, with 12 stones remaining, all under 3 feet. THE DRUIDS CIRCLE of Ulverston and BIRKRIGG (a rare concentric ring, featuring 20 outer and 12 inner stones) lie on the south Cumbrian coast. GAMELANDS CIRCLE is a larger affair, originally of 42 stones, and can be found at the foot of Knott Hill, east of the M6.

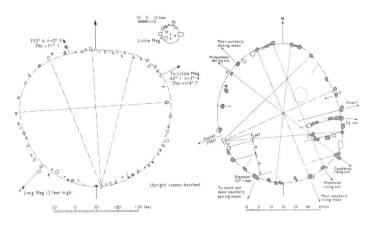

Above left and facing page: Long Meg and her Daughters (A. Thom). The 69 granite 'daughters' are arranged in a 359ft wide Type-B flattened circle (see page 13). Above right and below: Castlerigg stone circle, Keswick, a 108ft wide Type-A flattened circle with strong astronomical alignments.

WALES & ANGLESEY
refuge of the Druids

Wales once had a thriving megalithic culture, and the stones still carry hundreds of legends of giants and associations with King Arthur.

CERRIG DUON ('Black Rock') is one of many rings in South Wales. The ovoid shape is about 70 ft in diameter, with an avenue heading northeast. Its mighty Maen Mawr stone weighs about ten tons and sits north of the circle; visible from a great distance, it still serves as a marker for travellers coming up from the Tawe Valley.

Heading northwest, high up in the Preseli Mountains, BEDD ARTHUR (Arthur's Grave) is an oval arrangement of small stones, overlooking the rocky outcrop of Carn Meini. The idea of the oval Bluestone 'horseshoe' at Stonehenge may have originated here. East of Aberystwyth, at YSBYTY CYNFYN near the famous Devil's Bridge, a Christianised stone circle is now part of the church wall. The tallest stone is 11 ft, and surviving menhirs mark the boundary of what could have been the largest megalithic site in Wales.

The DRUID'S CIRCLE, just south of Penmaenmawr in North Wales, sits high on a wind-blown stretch of moorland. It was described by Edward Llwyd in 1695 as "the most remarkable monument in all Snowden". The perfectly formed MOEL TY UCHAF (*see p. 12*), 'Hill of the Highest House', 1,375 ft above Merioneth, is, according to Keith Critchlow, "perhaps the most geometrically sophisticated of all Neolithic structures".

Anglesey is remembered as the last stronghold of the Druids. Its most famous surviving circle site—BRYN CELLI DDU—dates to 4800 BC and is now a chambered tomb oriented to the summer solstice sunrise, but once had an oval megalithic ring with about 17 stones (*lower opposite*).

Above: Druid's Circle in North Wales. An oval arrangement of some 30 granite stones.

Above: Bryn Celli Ddu, Anglesey, in 1847 and 150 years later, after restoration.

Above: Henblas Dolmen, Anglesey. These stones are latticed with thick veins of quartz.

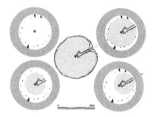

Above: Phases of Bryn Celli Ddu, anticlockwise from top left, showing stone circle.

Above: "The great Temple & Grove of the Druids at Trerdrew in Anglesea," known today as the Bryn Gwyn complex, as recorded by Stukeley in his Itinerarium Curiousum in 1725.

LOWLAND SCOTLAND
and the borders

Southwest Scotland boasts many circles in a variety of styles (the southeast has only one of note—BORROWSTONE RIG, *shown opposite*).

The oval shaped TWELVE APOSTLES near Dumfries is the largest in Scotland and the seventh largest in Britain. Mostly now destroyed, it was once nearly 300ft across. GLENQUICKEN is a circular ring of 29 stones with a chunky granite pillar at its centre. Described by Aubrey Burl as 'the most perfect centre-stone circle in the British Isles,' it was here that a 'man of uncommon size' was unearthed in the 1800s.

TORHOUSEKIE is just as delightful, sitting on a raised terrace with 19 graded granite stones. It has been compared to Aberdeenshire's recumbent circles, although it probably dates from an earlier period.

Around Kilmartin, the small TEMPLEWOOD arrangement looks like a circle of gravestones; rightly so, as it is an ancient burial site (*see opposite*).

Loch Tay in Perthshire is surrounded by megalithic circles including CROFT MORAIG (*shown below, after Piggott & Simpson*), the ACHARN FALLS, KINNELL OF KILLIN, LEYS OF MARLEE, and FORTINGALL. Fortingall is a sunken triple circle with some cup marked stones, overlooked by Mount Schiehallion, or *Sìdh Chailleann*, which translates as 'Fairy Hill'.

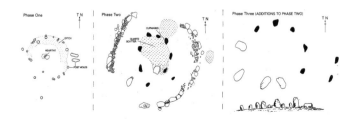

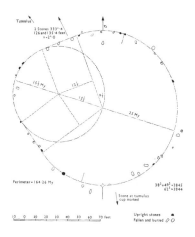

Tumulus

2 Stones 333° 4
126 and 135° 4 feet
h = 2° 0

15½ My   12½

15½   9½

25 My

Perimeter = 164·26 My

38³ + 49² = 3845
62² = 3844

Stone at tumulus
cup marked

10 0 10 20 30 40 50 60 70 feet

Upright stones ●
Fallen and buried ⌀ ○

*Left: Geometrical analysis of Borrowstone
Rig (A. Thom).   Above: LUNDIN LINKS
in Fife. Once four stones, it is typical of a
megalithic 'Four Poster' style found all over
Scotland.   Below: Templewood stone circle,
in the extraordinary Kilmartin valley. It
began life as a circle of twenty stones of local
schist, and is dated to 3500 BC.*

SCOTTISH HIGHLANDS
tracking the southernmost moon

Crossing into the Scottish Highlands reveals a few small circles, such as the one at KILLIN, Perthshire (*shown below right*). Further north, there are over 150 recumbent stone circles in Aberdeenshire (there were once many more). Built high up with a clear southern horizon, many of them feature a massive recumbent block, often up to 60 tons, oriented to the southwest (*e.g. below left, at DYCE*). Two upright 'flankers' sit either side creating a horizontal 'altar' or *false horizon*, which frames the path of the low midsummer, southernmost setting moon (*see opposite*). Some circles don't fit this astronomical scheme, and echo earlier examples dating to between 2700–2000 BC. Many are burial sites with a cairn in the ring. MIDMAR KIRK is now in a churchyard.

Nearly 200 geometric carved stone spheres have been found in the Grampian area in the vicinity of stone circles. Tetrahedra, cubes, octahedra and icosahedra all fit into one's palm. Some, like the famous TOWIE BALL (*inset top left*), have beautiful spiral patterns.

Around Inverness, construction style changes. Several stone circles and ring cairns cluster at the head of Loch Ness. CLAVA CAIRNS are three burial sites with a SW orientation, all surrounded by 12 stones. CORRIMONY, to the southwest, is similar but larger. The simple DRUIDTEMPLE is a perfect 'egg shaped ring' (*opposite top right*). Further north, rings get smaller, until we come to the giants in the islands.

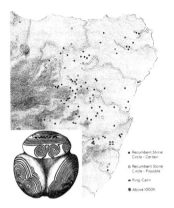

Above: Aubrey Burl's map of recumbent circles in Aberdeenshire; originally there were over 300.

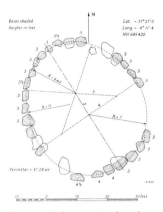

Above: 3-4-5 Pythagorean triangles in the inner ring of the Druidtemple in Inverness (A. Thom).

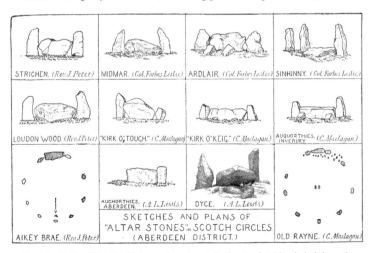

STRICHEN. (Rev. J. Peter.) MIDMAR. (Col. Forbes Leslie.) ARDLAIR. (Col. Forbes Leslie.) SINHINNY. (Col. Forbes Leslie.)

LOUDON WOOD. (Rev. J. Peter.) "KIRK O' TOUGH." (C. Maclagan.) "KIRK O' KEIG." (C. Maclagan.) AUQUORTHIES, INVERURY. (C. Maclagan.)

AIKEY BRAE. (Rev. J. Peter.) AUCHORTHIES, ABERDEEN. (A. L. Lewis.) DYCE. (A. L. Lewis.)

SKETCHES AND PLANS OF "ALTAR STONES" IN SCOTCH CIRCLES. (ABERDEEN DISTRICT.)

OLD RAYNE. (C. Maclagan.)

Above: A selection of Aberdeenshire's recumbent stone circles showing their 'altars' which frame the midsummer moonset, particularly its southernmost setting which occurs every 18.6 years.

39

THE SCOTTISH ISLANDS
the high art perfected

Most of the Scottish islands have stone circles. Some are small, lost, or hidden, others magnificent in their scale and beauty. On Arran, AUCHAGALLON CAIRN and LAMLASH are two modest examples (15 and 7 stones respectively). MACHRIE MOOR (*below left*) has several rings.

On Mull, two 8 ft menhirs remain of the BALLISCATE stone circle. On the south coast the 9 large stones of LOCHBUIE stand in the 'Field of the Druids'. In the south of Skye, NA CLACHAN BHREIGE (false stones) sits amid beautiful scenery with three tall standing stones, and one fallen.

In the Outer Hebrides, the cruciform site of CALLANISH (*opposite top*) dominates the Isle of Lewis, its four avenues meeting at a circle of 12 impressive blades forming a Type-A flattened circle and enclosing a 15 ft central menhir. The nearby concentric circle of CNOC FILLIBHEAR BHEAG and the smaller GHARRAIDH are also worth a visit.

The Orkney circles share Callanish's mystical quality, attracting hardened megalithomaniacs. The RING OF BRODGAR (*opposite centre, and in the background of 2800 BC Maes Howe, below right*) is the largest in Scotland. Once known as *The Temple of the Sun*, its smaller companion, the STONES OF STENNESS (*opposite bottom*), was called *The Temple of the Moon*.

Callanish, on the Isle of Lewis, has the form of a Celtic cross (a circle with four avenues).

The Ring of Brodgar; 341 ft (104m) wide, 2500BC. A nearby site, the Ness of Brodgar, dates to 3300BC.

The Stones of Stenness; the henge was cut 2m into solid rock, removing 18,000 cubic metres of stone.

IRISH CIRCLES
justified and ancient

The oldest stone circles in the British Isles are found in Sligo, NW Ireland. The area around Knocknarea mountain has 1,450 megalithic tombs and 22 low lying 'Boulder Circles', like the one at the CARROWMORE complex (*opposite, top right*). Here, Swedish archaeologists have pushed construction back as far as 7490 BC, the oldest in Europe, long before the more famous sites appear in the Boyne Valley.

The mighty passage grave of NEWGRANGE in Co. Meath (*opposite bottom*) was once surrounded by a circle of stones which may have predated the main structure; some still remain. Nearby, KNOWTH and DOWTH (also passage graves) are each propped up by circles of beautifully carved stones.

South of Dublin in Co. Wicklow are the ATHGREANY PIPER STONES with a midsummer sunrise alignment and one unusually large cup-mark. BROADLEAS, 105 ft across, is oval, like many in Cumbria.

Southern Ireland has many stone rings of different sizes and shapes. DROMBEG in Cork is one of 80 that resemble the Aberdeenshire recumbents, only smaller. Many Limerick circles, like the tiny LISSYVIGGEEN in Co. Kerry or the enormous LIOS CIRCLE near Bruff, are set within an earthen bank. KEALKIL is utterly charming.

In Co. Donegal, Northern Ireland, the beautifully set BELTANY RING dates from the end of the British circle-building era around 1400 BC. Cup-marked, it was once a tomb, and aligns to the May Day sunrise. In Ulster, there are several low rings of small stones built after 1900 BC. These are multiple sites with cairns in their centres, or nearby, and some have avenues, such as BEAGHMORE STONE CIRCLES in Co. Tyrone.

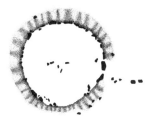

Above: Castleruddery, County Wicklow, with outer bank and eastern entrance.

Above: Circle 7, Carrowmore, with central small dolmen, & Knocknarea Mountain with cairns (Brennan, 1982).

Above: Greidle, Co. Down, N. Ireland. Six stones of a court remain, two leading to a gallery.

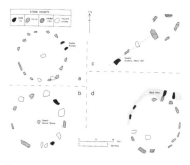

Above: Four stone circles from Cork. a: Carrigagulla SW; b. Currebeha; c. Knockraheen; d. Carrigagrenane (from Burl, after Barber, 1972).

Above: Entrance stone at Newgrange.
Below: Newgrange before excavation.

GERMANY & SCANDINAVIA
burials for the dead

Scandinavia is famous for its majestic stone ships. Shaped like longboats, many of these circle-type constructions are grave sites. However, the iconic ALE'S STONES (*below*) in Skåne, Sweden, shows no trace of burial. It aligns to winter solstice sunrise and summer solstice sunset. A stone ship was added in the 10th century to an existing Bronze Age mound at SKIBSSAETNING. It is common in this part of the world for sites to date from the Neolithic up to the Viking era, as megalith builders suffered less from Christians vandalising and re-dedicating their sites.

There are twelve known circles in Norway, the most important being HUNN GRAVFELT on the Østfold 'Prehistoric Road'. At this site are nine stone circles and a number of burial mounds dating to about 1200 BC. On one of the stones is a runic carving. LUNDEBY TINGSTED is another fine example consisting of three small circles.

Poland has some fantastic sites. Officially dated to around 300 AD the ODRY RING COMPLEX in Pomorskie (*opposite, centre*) is now thought to have been built around 2000 BC. Twelve stone circles range from 15m to 33m in diameter and comprise between 16 and 29 stones.

Germany is more known for its chambered dolmens, but in the North some stone circles (Ger. *steinkreis*) lie hidden in the woods. BOITIN STEINTANZ (*steintanz* = 'stone dance') in Western Pomerania is a group of four stone circles. Nearby NETZEBAND is another example.

Above: 1880s reconstruction of
ancient burial site, ROESKILDE,
Denmark, typical to the area.

Below: Odry, Poland, has many burial mounds
and twelve 15-33m stone circles, each of 16 to 29
stones, 20-70cm high, many with central menhirs.
Three rings point to winter solstice sunrise,
another three to summer solstice sunrise.

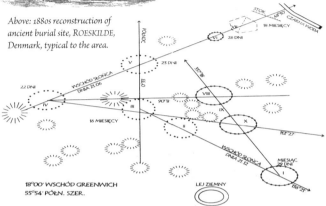

Facing page: Swedish stone
boats at WISKEHÄRAD,
Halland, and Ale's Stones,
c.500 AD, C Hilfeling, 1777.

Left: 1880s watercolour
by Olof Hermelin of the
GREBY PREHISTORIC
GRAVE FIELDS, Sweden,
with battlefield burial
mounds, stone circles and
single monoliths.

France, Spain & Portugal

all shapes and sizes

Some of the oldest and largest megaliths in the world are at CARNAC, Brittany (*opposite centre*). A vast complex, of global significance, its approximately 45 circles (French *cromlechs,* from the Welsh *crwmllech*) can be egg-shaped, horse-shoes, or rectangular or square.

Although many French cromlechs are often differ from their British counterparts, in the early 19th century an English-style oval on the ISLET OF BENIGUET in Finistere was illustrated showing 12 stones in the Cornish style (*see opposite*). Also off the north coast, in a tidal zone on the ISLE OF CHAUCEY, is a curious circle of 40 stones, completely submerged at high tide. In the south, LACAM DE PEYRARINES in Languedoc is a very British affair: a huge oval 340 by 290 feet wide with a central menhir. Nearby, LACAM DE LA RIGALDERIE is slightly smaller with 36 stones.

The border area between France and Spain has many small cromlechs, often clustered together, with some dating from well into the Iron Age. Hundreds are dotted across the Pyrenees. On the western extreme a notable 'four poster' called MENDILUZE HARRESPILA in Pais Vasco is officially dated to around 800 BC.

Portugal has some spectacular sites (*below, and see caption opposite*).

Above: Early 19th century drawing of a stone circle on ILE BENIGUET, Finistere, France, now destroyed.

Top right: Dolmen at Crucuno, Carnac. Above: Menec West Cromlech, Carnac. Dated to 4500 BC, it is perhaps the earliest prototype, egg-shaped ring. It is attached to multiple stone rows.

Almendres I
(Neolítico antigo-médio)

Almendres II
(Neolítico médio)

Almendres III
(Neolítico final)

Above and right: Portugal has some of the finest and oldest cromlechs in Europe. Near Evora is the 8,000-year-old CROMELEQUE DOS ALMENDRES with rounded granite stones, and nearby dolmens. From this 92-stone circle the midwinter sun rises above the 8ft MENHIR DO ALMENDRES, 1km to the southeast. Two similar cromlechs called PORTELA DE MOGOS and VALE DO MEIO are located nearby; as is the square XEREZ (opposite), dated to 4000 BC.

MALTA & NORTH AFRICA
and the Senegambian circles

Malta is home to many temples: MNAJDRA and HAGAR QIM (*see p. 58*), and the Xaghra complex on the isle of GOZO (*see opposite*). Further south, in Morocco, the MSOURA ring can be found near Asilah. This is a huge ellipse, 195 ft (59.29m) by 185 ft (56.18m); 168 stones survive out of the original 175. A later, part-excavated tumulus sits in its centre.

Near Cyrenaica in Libya a stone circle was recorded in 1882, and other trilithons and dolmens litter the north African coast. Hundreds of prehistoric tumuli, stelae and megalithic structures are located about 60 miles west of Abu Simbel in southern Egypt. A small egg-shaped stone ring called NABTA PLAYA (*see below*) was found in 1974 in the Nubian Desert; at 7,000 years old, it is the oldest so far discovered in Africa.

There are 93 stone circles in Senegal and Gambia, dated 300 BC–1600 AD, and divided between SINE NGAYENE and WANAR in Senegal, and WASSU and KERBATCH in Gambia (*below right*). The laterite stones are cylindrical or polygonal with the heaviest weighing around 7 tons.

In the Mpumalanga region of South Africa, a striking and ancient 100 ft stone circle called ADAM'S CALENDAR was discovered in 2003.

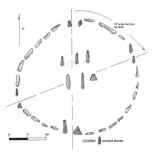

Left: Nabta Playa is a Type 1 egg-shaped circle, dated to 5000 BC, aligned to the summer solstice sunrise. Below: Circles at Kerbatch, Gambia.

Above: Msoura, in northern Morocco, is a stone ellipse constructed using a 12-35-37 Pythagorean triangle (similar to over 30 British examples).

Above: 19th century photograph of megalithic trilithons in Libya, resembling those of Stonehenge. Another one can be found at ELKEB, near Tripoli.

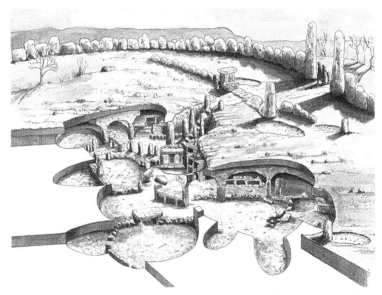

Above: Illustrated reconstruction by Prof. Caroline Malone of the circular hypogeum at Xaghra, close to the nearby larger site of Ggantija on the Maltese island of Gozo. The site dates from 4100-2500 BC. Around a quarter of a million bones and objects from 800 individuals were discovered in underground chambers below the stone circle during excavations in the 1980s. The site is now closed to the public.

THE AMERICAS
circles north and south

In North America, hundreds of stone chambers, dolmens and menhirs stretch across New England and New York state. Within this hidden megalithic landscape are two stone circles, BURNT HILL (*opposite, top left*) and THE DRUIDS CIRCLE. In 1602, Spanish explorer Sebastian Vizcaino visited Catalina Island, California, with chronicler Father Torquemada and described a ceremonial complex "formed by a large circle of long stones pointing upward toward the mid-day sun".

The 'Stonehenge of the Amazon', CALÇOENE MEGALITHIC OBSER-VATORY, is located on a hilltop near Calçoene, Amapa, Brazil. Here, 127 blocks of granite, up to 11 ft tall, are spaced at regular intervals around the hill, like a crown. The 100ft circle is thought to have been constructed by the Amapán people between the 1st and 10th century AD. It has a winter solstice sunrise alignment.

SILLUSTANI, near Lake Titicaca in Peru, is well known for its huge hilltop funerary towers called 'Chulpas' (*opposite top right*). On the plains below are several astronomically-aligned stone circles built by the Kolla (a pre-Inca culture) between 100 AD and 1600 AD. The largest, at 34ft, is INTIWATANA (*shown opposite*), which translates as "to moor the sun".

Above: Burnt Hill, Heath, Massachussetts. Inspiration for H.P. Lovecraft's Sentinel Hill in The Dunwhich Horror: 'Oldest of all are the great rings of rough-hewn stone columns on the hilltops, but these are more generally attributed to the Indians than to the settlers'.

Opposite Page: Calçoene, Brazil. Above: Intiwatana, Peru, in 1877, one of six stone circles at Sillustani. Above, top right: The plateau is dominated by Chulpas—megalithic round towers.

Karahunge & Middle East
lost circles of the Bible

Armenia boasts one of the oldest, most impressive circles in the world. Called Zorats Karer or Karenish by the locals, and widely known as Armenia's Stonehenge, Karahunge has 223 standing stones that vary between 2 ft and 9 ft tall and weigh up to 10 tons (*see opposite*). 80 stones have circular holes drilled through them, 37 are still standing.

There are 39 mentions in the Bible of Gilgal, a 'circle of standing stones'. In one account, after miraculously crossing the river Jordan, Joshua orders the Israelites to take twelve large stones from the river bed, one for each tribe, and place them at Gilgal 'in memory'. Gilgal has been identified with the village of Jiljilia, about 8m north of Bethel.

In present-day Israel, the submerged site of Atlit Yam (*opposite bottom*) near Haifa dates from 6900–6300 BC and is the earliest known evidence for an agro-pastoral-marine subsistence system on the Levantine coast. A stone semicircle containing seven half-ton monoliths was discovered at a depth of 8–12m. The stones have cup marks carved into them, and surround a freshwater spring.

Above: Karahunge (speaking stones). 17 of the stones align to sunrise and sunset at the solstices and equinoxes, and 14 to lunar extremes. Russian prehistorian Professor Paris Herouni analysed a prominent holed stone and found that it aligned to Deneb, the brightest star of Cygnus, c.5500 BC.

Opposite page: Two illustrations of the stone circle complex in DARABGIRD, Iran. The lozenge-shaped stones are similar to those at Avebury and other sites in Britain.

Left: Reconstruction of the submerged stone circle at Atlit Yam, Haifa, Israel.

FAR EAST & DOWN UNDER
from India to Australia

Northern Pakistan is home to several stone circles. Local legend has it that the 30-stone Asota ring at Kalula (*opposite top*) was erected by *Ashoka* (Buddha) so he could meditate at one each day of the month.

India has a rich megalithic heritage, including around 300 prehistoric low stone circles in Junapani, Maharashtra state, dated to 1000 BC. In the Dekkan region, stone circles were still being built in the 1800s (*see example below*), while the massive Mudumal Stone Circle in Telangana (*opposite, centre right*) is now thought to date to 5000 BC.

In Northern Japan, about 30 stone rings were built by the Jomon culture between 2400 BC and 1000 BC, a fine example can be seen at Oshoro, where there is a 22 by 33m oval, with an internal circle.

In Australia, at Wurdi Youang, Victoria, a 165 ft circle, possibly 11,000 years old, of over 100 basalt boulders aligns to the sunsets on the solstices and equinoxes. At Mullumbimby, in New South Wales, two extremely ancient circles were once linked by an avenue (*see opposite*).

Asota (Kalula) stone circle in Northern Pakistan—one of many in this area.

Above left: Dolmen and circles at PULLICONDAH, near Madras, India.   Above right: Mudumal Stone Circle in Telangana, India, is 7,000 years old and has a cup-mark carving of the Big Dipper.

Above: Mullumbimby, New South Wales, Australia. 181 standing stones, on a 100m long boomerang-shaped mound, once formed two circles linked by an avenue, overlooking Byron Bay. The site is now thought to be extremely ancient. A large, partly excavated tumulus is located less than 100 yards away.

MODERN STONE CIRCLES
the renaissance of megalithomania

Few stone circles were constructed in Europe after 1000BC. However, in Indonesia and other remote nations, some tribes still get together and quarry, transport and build megalithic structures.

The first modern circle in Britain was probably inspired by John Aubrey. On midsummer's day in 1717 the Irish author J. J. Toland held a meeting for Druids in London on PRIMROSE HILL, London (*see opposite*), and established *The Ancient Druid Order*. Later in the 18th century, this inspired Iolo Morganwg [1747-1826] to form the *Gorsedd of the Bards of the Isle of Britain*. Some years later again, around 1800, a ring of stones was constructed around the great Pontypridd "rocking stone" in Wales, due to its popularity as a pagan ritual site (*see opposite*).

Since the 1960s, individuals, festivals (*e.g. opposite top right*) and organisations the world over have built an estimated 200 stone circles. There is even one in the middle of a roundabout in MILTON KEYNES, UK. Other notable examples include: HAM HILL in Somerset, HILLY FIELDS in Lewisham, London, and MARYHILL war memorial in Washington, US, a concrete replica of Stonehenge which has nevertheless been found to have interesting acoustic properties. Megalith builders such as Rob Roy and Ivan McBeth have constructed numerous rings using ancient techniques from England to New England.

The prehistoric sites detailed in this book may represent a golden age of astronomy, earth mysteries and technological prowess. However, with a new wave of megalithomania sweeping the planet, more will surely be built, leaving future archaeologists and antiquarians just as baffled as we are now! The power of the ancients has come full circle.

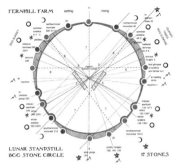

FERNHILL FARM

LUNAR STANDSTILL
BGG STONE CIRCLE

17 STONES

Above: Design for a stone circle for the 2006 Big
Green Gathering by J. Martineau & S. Kirwan.

Left: Plan for a stone circle from the famous
Druid revival meeting on Primrose Hill in 1792.

PONTYPRIDD ROCKING STONE, Glamorgan. In 1795, a gorsedd meeting took place around the huge
slab of natural slate stone (the Maen Chwyf). The circle was a later addition. In 1899 a formal plan
for future stone circles was produced. Until recently, one was constructed at each annual Eisteddfod so
there are now numerous modern stone circle across Wales (and even Hungary and Patagonia).

A GLOBAL CULTURE
what were the ancients up to?

No-one knows why ancient peoples went to such lengths to drag, cut and raise the stones we have seen in these pages, and yet their circles and temples show a sophistication at odds with the crude materials they worked with. Some people have suggested that the reason we find the same early building styles all around the world is that there was once a global civilisation, of whom almost no trace remains today.

Mnajdra Temple, Malta, c.3500BC